I0421454

This Belongs To:

Published by Two Rivers Publishing
TwoRiversPublishing.com

www.ingramcontent.com/pod-product-compliance
Lightning Source LLC
Chambersburg PA
CBHW060427290526
45791CB00002B/893
9781075983405